INTERNSHIP COURSE WORKBOOK

DR. ANTHONY BORGESE

BROOKLYN, NEW YORK
ASSOCIATE PROFESSOR
CITY UNIVERSITY OF NEW YORK

Custom Publishing

New York Boston San Francisco
London Toronto Sydney Tokyo Singapore Madrid
Mexico City Munich Paris Cape Town Hong Kong Montreal

Printed in the United States of America

17 2024

2009840023

MP

**Pearson
Custom Publishing**
is a division of

www.pearsonhighered.com

ISBN 10: 0-558-31255-1
ISBN 13: 978-0-558-31255-8

Dedication

For the two loves of my life:

My beautiful wife Renata, and my

Heart and soul, Angelina

Acknowledgements

I would like to thank my friend and mentor, Dr. Stuart Schulman. Through his guidance and insight, I was able to design a workbook that is practical to the student's of today. In addition, as a pioneer of the internship course, many of his assignments can be seen throughout the workbook.

I would also like to acknowledge my colleagues. Dr. Graziano, who was a big supporter of this desperately needed project, and an excellent proofreader. Also, my colleagues that teach internship courses: Professor's Marshall, Bufano, and Deutsch. We now have something we can use! To Foglia, no more copying! Finally, to my Hospitality colleagues in the department: thank you for your help and support.

I would also like to thank all of my past, present, and future students at KCC. It is because of all of you that I have assembled these assignments over the past decade. Use the information found within to capture your dream internship/career!

Table of Contents

I. **Preparation**

II. **Participation**

Introduction

Welcome to your internship. Internships are provided as a way for students to gain practical, on the job training and skills into their chosen field of study. Throughout your academic studies, you have been learning the theoretical side of your chosen field, gaining valuable insight into how things are done in that career area. Internships provide a different type of training because you get to see and experience the actual work that is performed on a daily basis. The experience you gain from participating in an internship allows you to build a skill set that will ultimately make you more desirable in the job market.

Not all internship courses are created equally, but most internship courses do have common components. For example, all internship fieldwork will have you perform duties at an organization that specializes in your chosen career field. However, how you obtain the internship depends on the course you are in, and the requirements set by the professor. Some internship programs require the student to create his/her own program and obtain the internship him/herself, whereas other internship programs might use pre-established contacts in order to place students. Obviously, knowing how your internship course operates is very important.

At the City University of New York, there are a variety of different internship programs. You may be a student in a Hospitality Program at Kingsborough, hoping to do an internship at a New York City Hotel, or you could be an online Business student in the SPS hoping to land an internship in a business-related company. Either way, there are other skills you must master that are part of the overall internship experience. The following pages provide you with the content that will allow you to be successful with finding, landing, and participating successfully in your internship. Good luck!

Knowing Your Requirements

The first few things you need to understand are the course requirements for your internship. Requirements come in the form of: 1) the number of work hours you must put into your internship, 2) whether or not there is a classroom component, 3) how you will deal with problems, etc. Some professors of internship courses require students to find their own internship, whereas professors in other internship courses will use their industry contacts to place students at an internship location, after going through an informal or formal interview. Some internship courses might have a classroom component added to the course, whereas others might require a heavy one-on-one interaction with your professor. Knowing what the requirements are for your internship is of vital importance.

At the City University of New York, if you are in the Online Baccalaureate Program, BUS 440, then it is up to you to find your own internship. You must first fill out an Internship Proposal Form that outlines your internship, and it must be approved by your professor BEFORE you start your internship. Failure to get your internship approved may result in no credit being issued.

If you are in a career program at the City University of New York, more than likely, you will have the option of finding your own internship, or having your professor place you at an internship. Either way, both online and career students have a classroom component attached to the internship course. In the classroom component you will learn more skills that will make you more marketable to employers.

Course Overview

This course is a practical application of the student's academic studies via field experience, also known as internship. Students gain valuable work experience in their chosen field, as well as a sense of personal accomplishment. Internships offer students an opportunity to apply classroom knowledge in a professional environment.

Many advantages result from this field experience, including:

- Establishment of professional contacts
- Exploration of career options
- Valuable work experience including skills and aptitudes necessary for success
- Sense of personal accomplishment

CUNY SPS

Students are required to find their own internship placement and submit a formal internship proposal for approval before they start their internship. Ideally, internship hours should be a minimum of 150 hours to a maximum of 500 hours. Additionally, students must maintain a journal/blog of their internship experience, complete all of the assignments as outlined, and submit a 25 page term paper.

Student interns will conduct themselves in a professional manner at all times. This includes the development of respectful and cooperative relationships with the site supervisor and other employees at the sponsoring organization. The student will establish and maintain regular and punctual work hours, as outlined in the internship proposal, and will conduct him or herself in an ethical manner, conforming to the sponsoring organization's policies and procedures while executing the specific duties and responsibilities of the internship position. Failure to comply with the sponsoring organization's policies may result in suspension or termination of the internship.

There are a variety of **weekly assignments** for this course that are accessed by signing into the course on Blackboard through the portal. First, you will have regular, weekly assignments that are accessible through the Assignments Menu on the left hand side in Blackboard. Read the assignment, and complete the assignment by uploading your file through the submission link at the bottom of the individual assignment page. All files should have your last name and the assignment number. For example, Borgese_assignment1.

Discussion Board or DB. There will be at least one DB every week. In order to participate, click on the Discussion Board menu to the left and read through the DB topic for the week. Once you are ready to respond, you can click on the topic link and then on the Add New Thread button. Type in a subject line and then your response and thoughts to the topic and then click Submit. Your posting should now be visible to everyone in the course. You must post at least two times every week. The first posting is your response to the DBT and the second post is a response to another students' posting. These responses must be well thought out. Responses like: I agree, and Yes, that's right are not acceptable. You must say why you agree or disagree about…, etc.

Wiki's: Wiki's are not required to post to, but it is a good idea that we can put something together that might help each other out. The main Wiki for the semester is about helpful tips you might have and want to share with each other. For example, maybe something you did on a job interview really worked for you, or maybe you want to give advice on something to avoid. In order to participate in the Wiki, click on the Tools menu and then Wiki Tool. You should see the topic already posted there, and you may leave a comment, or start a new comment by clicking on either of those links.

Journals/Blogs: Weekly journal entries are required for this course. Each journal entry should be a minimum of 100 words per week and could relate to everything that happens to you throughout the course. This may include searching for the internship, interviewing, what occurred during your internship, etc. In order to post your journal/blog, click on the Tools menu to the left, then on the Blog Tool link. Click on the new entry link (upper right hand corner) in order to post your journal/blog. Make your blog titles your name and the date of the week that the journal covers. For example, "Angelina's Blog June 1-7, 2010". Type up your journal entry and then click on save.

Again, all of these assignments are weekly assignments, except for the Wiki, which is optional, but beneficial. If you have any questions, at any time throughout the semester, please feel free to email me your professor.

CUNY-Career Programs

Students have a choice of finding their own internship, or being placed at an internship location by your professor. Usually, students must have a resume before being sent to an interview for an internship. Students are required to do a minimum of 100 hours at the internship. Additionally, students are required to fulfill the classroom components of the course, as well as the exercises and assignments throughout this workbook.

Student interns will conduct themselves in a professional manner at all times. This includes the development of respectful and cooperative relationships with the site supervisor and other employees at the sponsoring organization. The student will establish and maintain regular and punctual work hours, as outlined in the internship proposal, and will conduct him or herself in an ethical manner, conforming to the sponsoring organization's policies and procedures while executing the specific duties and responsibilities of the internship position. Failure to comply with the sponsoring organization's policies may result in suspension or termination of the internship.

Since your class is a traditional, face-to-face course, you will meet with your professor on a weekly basis. At the beginning of the course, there is a variety of paperwork that needs to be filled out and processed in order for you to proceed with your internship. The very first form you need to fill out is the Internship Pledge form. (Back of the workbook) The internship pledge form provides your professor with a variety of information including: what type of internship you are looking for. Your professor uses the information you provide on this form to match you up with the best available internship, so be as detailed and as honest as possible.

You are required to attend class once each week, and you must work out a schedule with your internship provider to perform your internship hours. Classroom hours are spent learning a variety of career skills that are important to not only obtaining and being successful on your internship, but providing you with the tools necessary for having a successful career in the future.

Faculty Responsibilities

Your professor acts as a liaison between you and your internship. If you are an SPS student, your professor must approve all potential internship positions as worthy of academic credit and approve all internship proposals. Such determination shall be made based on the type of work to be performed, and by the contribution the internship will make to the student's learning experience.

If you are a student in a career program, then your professor is your lifeline between you and your internship supervisor. More than likely, your professor has placed you in an internship by utilizing departmental or his/her own industry contacts. These are contacts that have been developed over a long period of time, and are vital to the professor, CUNY, and the future of the internship program. You carry with you the reputation of both the institution and the professor. If any problems should arise, your professor will be the advocate between you and your internship provider in settling any and all problems.

The faculty supervisor is responsible for monitoring the student's activities during the duration of the internship. This monitoring may include: contacting the student's internship supervisor to check on the student's progress, meeting with the student, as necessary throughout the internship process, grading course assignments, evaluating the internship proposal and term paper, and assessing a grade for the overall internship experience.

Your faculty supervisor is also responsible for teaching the classroom portion of the course. Classroom content includes: resume writing, job searching, interviewing skills and overall career development. It is the goal of your faculty supervisor to have you leave the course with enough confidence to find a job within your chosen field.

Internship Proposal

For students who must obtain their own internship

The proposal serves as a formal agreement among the student, the sponsoring organization, and the faculty supervisor. It should describe the internship in sufficient detail so as to avoid subsequent confusion and misunderstanding. Therefore, the internship proposal should disclose any and all information concerning the internship that the parties feel are appropriate. As a minimum, the proposal should include statements concerning the following items.

Item 1: A statement of the internship objective: primarily to supplement the student's theoretical knowledge with a practical work experience. The specific related academic courses in which the theoretical knowledge was acquired should be identified as well.

Item 2: Brief statements of internship responsibilities.

*SPS Students: All internships require a 25 page term paper, as well as regular participation in the Blackboard course. In some instances, formal presentations may be required in addition to the term paper.

Site Supervisor: is responsible for directly or indirectly supervising internship activities and evaluating the student's performance.

Faculty Supervisor: He/she assigns the grade for the internship, provides course materials for the Blackboard site as well as counseling when required.

Other items: Number of hours to be worked and general description of the work schedule.

The student, site supervisor and faculty supervisor indicate agreement with the internship proposal by signing the internship proposal. A signed copy of the internship proposal indicates that the internship is worthy of academic credit and has been approved. Failure to have a signed copy of the internship proposal may result in a cancellation of the student's internship course enrollment.

Internship Proposal Form

For students who must obtain their own internship

This document is intended as a formal agreement among _____ (Intern), _____ (Faculty Supervisor), and _____ (Site Supervisor), concerning a 3-credit internship to be performed during the _____ semester of 20____ at _____ (Name of the Organization).

The objective of the internship is to supplement the intern's general theoretical knowledge of _____ (subject area) that has been gained through academic course work with a practical work experience. The internship objective will be achieved by the intern's performing the following specific duties:

1) _____
_____

2) _____
_____

3) _____
_____

(You may use the back of this form if necessary)

The internship will begin on _____ and conclude on _____. The intern will work for a total of ____ hours. The intern will maintain a daily journal documenting the duties performed. Upon completion of the internship, the intern will submit a paper summarizing his or her activities according to the course requirements.

The site supervisor will directly or indirectly supervise the internship activities, and evaluate the intern's performance using the Intern Evaluation Form provided.

The grade for the internship will be assigned by the faculty supervisor and will be based upon the following components and weights as specified by the supervising faculty member.

1) Classroom/Online Course Component   ____%
2) Site supervisor evaluation   ____%
3) Exams   ____%
4) Other:_____   ____%

_____ _____
(Faculty Supervisor Signature)   (Date)

_____
(Print Site Supervisor Name)

_____ _____
(Intern signature)   (Date)

_____ _____
(Site Supervisor signature)   (Date)

Resume Writing

A good resume is your first step towards obtaining a successful internship or job. Your resume introduces you to the perspective company for which you wish to work. A good resume contains valuable information about your and grabs the attention of the employer, thereby persuading the employer to call you in for an interview. Hence, a good resume gets "your foot in the door".

There is no universal format to writing a resume, however, there are some common threads found throughout most resumes. For example, your name and contact information should be clearly visible at the top of the resume. Cell phone numbers and emails addresses are commonly found as part of the contact information. **Tips**: 1) Do not use an email address that is offensive or personal. Create a free, professional email address on the Internet. 2) Make sure your voicemail message is clear and professional as well. What might be funny to you may not be funny to your prospective employer. You can always change your message after you get the job or internship.

The next part of the resume has traditionally been the professional goal or an objective of the job seeker. Whether or not this is a necessary part of your resume is up for debate. Recently, professional summaries have taken over for objectives. Professional summaries tend to be more useful for job seekers with a variety of work experience, whereas objectives should be used to specify the career the job seeker is hoping to achieve. For example, a good objective would be: To obtain a position in _____ (state the position) where my academic credentials, enthusiasm and diligence will lead to opportunities for professional growth.

Tips: 1) Tailor your objective to the position you are seeking. For example, if you have a marketing degree and are applying for a sales position, state the sales position, and not marketing, as your objective. 2) If you use a professional summary summarize yourself by using descriptive words such as: Adaptable, Ambitious, Analytical, Conscientious, Cooperative, Creative, Dependable, Determined, Disciplined, Energetic, Enthusiastic, Pleasant, Positive, Reliable, and Resourceful. You should, therefore, send a tailored resume to job or internship posting.

The order of the third common part of a resume is either education or work experience depending on your personal preference. If you have viable work experience in the career area for which you are applying, then the work experience section should definitely be next. If you do not have practical work experience in the career area, then the education section should be listed next. The education piece should list higher education either completed or near completion. For simplicity, you should list the name, and perhaps address, of your school, your major, the degree you obtained and the year you completed it. If you have not yet graduated, then add: Expected Date of Graduation: June 2010

Tips: 1) Be truthful as your education is easily verified. 2) Do not list your high school, unless that is your only education. 3) Add certification programs. 4) If you do not have much work experience, list the college courses that you have taken that relate to the job you are seeking.

Work experience, is probably the most important part of your resume. All human resources managers will tell you that nothing beats experience. First of all, you should start by listing your current job first and then list previous jobs in descending order. The name and location of the company, the dates you worked there and your title are the common beginnings to your work experience section. Next, you want to use bullet points to describe at least three (3) duties or responsibilities you performed in that position.

Tips: 1) Use action words to start off your bullet points. Directed, Managed, Led, Assigned, Allocated, Analyzed, Controlled, Created, Developed, Generated, Implemented, Increased, Organized, Supervised and Supported are a few common action words. 2) You should have increasing responsibilities as your career has moved forward, therefore put your strongest responsibilities first and the weakest toward the bottom.

The final common part of all resumes is the skills area. In this area you should list the skills that you possess that are necessary to be successful in the job or internship you are seeking to get. Skill sets come in a variety of different forms and may include: Microsoft Office Skills (Word, PowerPoint, Excel, Access), typing speed (if relevant to the job you are seeking), Internet research skills, language skills, demonstrated leadership skills, computer software skills (such as accounting software, or property management software).

Tips: 1) Look at the classified ad you are answering for clues as to what the employer is seeking in an applicant. Key words are the specific skills and requirements that MUST be on your resume in order for you to be considered for an internship/job. Human resources personnel now use resume tracking software to scan your resume to confirm that your resume contains the key words (skills/requirements) the company is interested in. If the classified ad calls for a hard-working, fast learner, with a strong sense of responsibility, then those are all keywords that you should be included on your resume. 2) If you have basic skills in any area, indicate that your skill level is basic rather than omitting it altogether. For example, you can speak Spanish, but cannot read it.

Finally, here are some general tips for all resumes. Remember, these are only tips and you are the ultimate arbiter of what goes onto your resume.

General Tips:

1) Keep it short and simple, a.k.a. the KISS method. While the debate rages on as to whether two page resumes are acceptable or not, my advice is: if you can't fit all of your accomplishments onto one page, think of the human resources person that must sift through all of the resumes he/she will receive, and you will realize that shorter is better.

2) Remember your Key Words
3) Keep your responsibilities and duties short and sweet and do not write a paragraph.
4) Do not put a period at the end of your bullet point statements.
5) Do not list references on your resume, but be prepared to list them on your job application.
6) Do not list or mention salaries, unless specifically asked to.
7) Avoid font sizes and styles that are difficult to read.
8) Use appropriate spacing between sections.
9) Only use bolding and capitalization to make something STAND OUT.
10) Proofread and use spell check before sending out your resume.
11) Try to avoid off-color paper.
12) Do not include a picture.
13) Do not put your resume in a binder or folder.
14) Do not list physical characteristics of height, weight, etc.
15) Don't lie.

Resume Worksheet: Before you start to construct your resume, make sure you have the following information. (Some of this information is only required on job applications, but it is better to gather the information now.)

- Contact information
- A professional email address
- The names and locations of the schools you have attended or certifying agencies who granted your certification
- The correct name of the degree, certification, or major field of study, the date you received the degree or certification
- The names and locations of all of the companies you have worked/interned for
- Your job title, duties and responsibilities at the companies you have worked/interned for
- The dates that you started and ended to work for all of the companies you worked/interned for
- The telephone numbers of the companies for which you worked
- All the skills you have acquired
- The relevant courses you have taken that pertain to the job/internship you are seeking
- Personal references, at least 3

Internship/Job Searching

Searching for an internship varies a little from searching for a job or career. However, there are a few similarities when searching for careers or internships. The term, "search", indicates that job seekers are going to go out and investigate the opportunities that are available to them. With that being said the question becomes; "Where do I go to start my internship or job search"? There are a variety of ways to search for an internship or a job, let's look at a few of them now.

1. **The Internet**: The Internet has become the biggest source of information for internships. A simple search on the Internet reveals thousands of web sites that are specifically designed to provide information on internship programs throughout the United States and the world. A word of caution, some of these web sites require a fee to join and some may not be reputable sources. However, if you do your due diligence, it should be obvious which web sites are disreputable. Common sense dictates that if an offer sounds too good to be true, then it probably is a scam.

2. **The Internet II (Company Web sites)**: The Internet also provides direct contact to the web sites of major corporations, which, in turn, will have internship information listed on their web sites. I am sure that you have thought about working for a specific company at one point or another. Well, look up that company on the Internet and when you get to its web site, type in "internship", or "internship program" into their search box located on their web site and you will be given the links to their internship program. Try it now at IBM.com or any company of your choice.

   There are a few advantages to going straight to a company's web site. First of all, the web site provides you with all of the information pertaining to the internship program. The web site will list the business areas where the company has available internships, a description of your duties, the hours, duration and seasons the internship occurs, and the eligibility requirements for the internship program. Students are sometimes shocked that internships at good companies can last for months, rather than hours.

3. **The Internet III (Online newspapers/employment databases)**: Gone are the days of looking for internships or jobs in the local newspaper. Even the almighty New York Times has partnered with Monster.com to administer its classified ad section. So, in this case, whether it is the local newspaper or an online employment agency, the Internet is a powerful source of information.

   All of these types of web sites work the same. When you get to the main page there are search fields that allow you to type in exactly what you are looking for. The more specific your information is, the better the results you will get. For example, the search term "hotel" will reveal millions of results, whereas the search term "front desk agent, NYC" will yield much more manageable results. The reason for this is because the search engine will show all of the results that it has which contains the search word that you used. That means that even if there is a classified ad for a law firm that was interviewing job seekers at the local hotel, then the search engine would consider that a match to the search term "hotel". So, be careful about the search terms you use.

4. **Networking**: If the Internet is the most powerful way to search for a job or internship, then networking must be the most useful. A majority of students find their internship through networking. Students speak to their professors, other students who may have already had an internship, career counselors, friends, family members, and a variety of other people that comprise a good network, in order to find an internship.

The important thing to remember is to always keep in contact with your network and keep their contact information handy. Social networking sites have allowed people to stay in touch with each other, but some job seekers have used social networking web sites to reach out to their friends in order to get jobs/internships.

Even though the Internet has made networking a little easier, nothing beats keeping in touch with your network via the telephone or good old fashioned face-to-face meetings. One simple way to build your network is to speak to your fellow students and ask where they are interning. Who knows, the company at which they are interning may need more interns, and you will have the inside track.

Your professor and career counselors are other good sources of possible job/internship opportunities. Oftentimes, companies looking to hire or take on an intern, will contact the local college or university in order to get access to college student-interns. Ask your professor if he/she knows of any job/internship opportunities, but most of all, make a trip to your school's career development office and speak to a career counselor regarding any possible internship/job opportunities.

Finally, family and friends are also a great way to build your network. Family members and friends with jobs are good resources as to who is hiring, or in need of interns, now. Some companies will even give their workers a bonus for recommending a friend or family member for a job. Usually, if you are hired after your family member or friend recommends you, and you stay on the job for 6 months to a year, the person that recommended you will get a monetary bonus, so it works out for everyone.

Cover Letters

The cover letter is important for a variety of reasons. First of all, it serves as your introduction to your prospective employer/internship provider. Different job seekers are at different points of their careers. You may be a student who is about to graduate and you have little or no work experience. At other points in your career you may be looking to change career paths. Either way, cover letters should highlight some of your career goals and aspirations.

As with your resume writing, use the KISS method: keep it short and simple. Cover letters should contain the following:

1. Contact information (Name, address and telephone/cell number)
2. A greeting (Dear Sir/Madam, Dear Human Resources Manager) followed by a colon (:)
3. A sentence specifying the position for which you are applying and where you learned about the job. (I am submitting my resume with consideration to the _____ (name of the position) advertised in _____ (where you learned about the position.)
4. A short paragraph as to why you are qualified for the position. (Job seekers without experience should list their academic achievements. Job seekers with experience should briefly write about their accomplishments throughout their career.)
5. An ending to the letter that calls for the prospective employer to take action. (Please call me for an interview at your earliest convenience.)
6. A closing. (Sincerely, etc.)
7. Your name printed out with your signature on top.

Some further hints: cover letters should always be sent, especially when instructed by classified ads. Make sure you tailor each cover letter to the job you are seeking. A marketing coordinator's position is clearly different from a sales and marketing position. Search the internet for cover letter samples. In this case, there are great cover letter samples out there that are specific to certain groups of job seekers. (Experienced, inexperienced, career transition, etc.) Be sure it is grammatically correct. There can be no spelling, usage, punctuation, or capitalization errors.

The following is a sample of a cover letter.

Sample Cover Letter

Your Name
804 East 10th Street
New York, NY 10010

Company ABC

Human Resources Department

52409 Fifth Avenue

New York, NY 10019

Dear Sir or Madam:

I am very interested in your Marketing Assistant position that was advertised on Craig's List. I am enclosing my resume for consideration.

As you can see from my resume, I will be graduating soon with a degree in _____ (list your major.) As part of my degree program, I completed an internship as a marketing assistant with _____ (list the company name.) I really enjoyed and benefitted from the experience. I learned a great deal coordinating the overall marketing efforts of the company, and I wish to build on my success. I have also taken a variety of marketing courses, and have gained valuable experience from all of them.

I am very excited about the possibility of working for your company, and I believe I will be an asset to your firm. Please contact me at: 718-555-5555 to arrange an interview at your earliest convenience.

Sincerely,

Angelina Borgese

Angelina Borgese

Interviewing

Congratulations, you did it! Your resume and cover letter landed you an interview. Unfortunately, for most students this now becomes a most stressful time. Questions run through your head at unbelievable speeds. Where do I start? What do I do now? My heart is racing. Ugh, my hands are sweaty! What do I wear? Where is the company located? How do I get there? How do I act? What do I say? What do I say? Someone help me man, what do I say?

Yes, being asked to come in for an interview can be a stressful time, but it doesn't have to be that way. Just like most things in life, if you are properly prepared, then there is nothing to worry about. This is the same for the interview process. Rather than just worrying about it, if you properly prepare yourself for the interview, then you will do fine. Keep in mind that this goes for the confident person as well. Be confident, not cocky or overconfident when going to an interview. Be sure to arrive on time.

There are a variety of things to do and not to do regarding the interview process, but if you take it step by step, as a process, you can be successful. When you sent in your resume, there was something about the classified ad that interested you, so the first thing to do, if you haven't done so already, is some research on the company. Most companies have web sites with links to its company history. Read through those links and get an idea of what the company is about. Don't be surprised if you are asked to name the C.E.O. of the company or about other company information.

Next, do some research on the company's core products and offerings. Do they sell a product or offer a service? Are the products luxury or generic items? Do they offer high-end generic services? Who are its customers? What is its corporate culture? How do they treat their employees? Many of these questions can be answered by doing some research on the company's web site. Even the questions that cannot be answered can still be asked when you get to the interview.

Finally, some other research you must do borders on the simplistic. Simple things like: where the company is located is often overlooked. Do you know how to get there? Do you know how long it will take you to get there? You would be surprised as to how many job/internship seekers leave this small detail out, only to arrive late to an interview, thereby ruining their chances to be hired.

The next step in your interview preparation process is to prepare the answers for some of the questions you will undoubtedly be asked. The following are some of the most generic interview questions that you should be prepared to answer:

1. Tell me about yourself.
2. What is your biggest weakness?
3. Why are you leaving your current job?

4. Where do you see yourself in 5 years?
5. How has school prepared you for work?
6. Why should we hire you?
7. Do you have any questions for me?

All of the above are generic questions that interviewers might ask in some way, shape or form. When you prepare your answers to these questions, always frame it within the context of an internship or work and joining the company. So, when the interviewer asks, "Tell me about yourself"? He doesn't want to hear what you do for fun, but rather how you can help the company. So, limit your answer to your school, your major, and any courses that you have taken that relate to the job/internship you are seeking. For example, "I am a junior at Baruch College, majoring in business. I have taken a variety of marketing courses which is what bring me here today. I would really love to intern with your company where I can learn more and possibly apply the skills that I have developed in school".

All interviewers will ask a question as to what you perceive as one of your weaknesses. The interviewer may not be as blunt as in the question above, but there will be a form of weakness question on your interview. When answering this question, always try to use a negative that is really a positive. What do I mean by this? Consider the following as an answer to the question of what my greatest weakness is. "I am very detail oriented and I always strive for perfection, and some people are not always comfortable with this". I turn the "weaknesses" of being detail oriented and a perfectionist into a problem that most employers can live with.

The question of why are you leaving your current job is not something that an internship interviewer would ask, but it is definitely a question that a job seeker will be asked. Interviewers want to know about why you are leaving a job and the answer you give is very important. No one wants to hear that you want more money, even though that may very well be the case. When answering this question stick to being positive about the possibility of being hired and do not be negative about your current job situation. For example, mention that there is no room for growth at the company you currently work for. This answer shows that you wish to grow in your career with the new company, but is not negative about the company you currently work for. There could be a variety of reasons why there is no room for growth at your present company.

Where do you see yourself down the road is another typical interview question that you should be prepared to answer. Interviewers want to hear your commitment level to the organization. They want to know that you want to grow with the company and not just take on a job just to get experience and put it on a resume. In addition, trying to be funny and saying that you would be in the interviewer's job is not appropriate either. When answering this question stick with growth and development responses. So, where do you see yourself in 5 years; learning more about the company, taking on more responsibility, and possibly moving into a supervisory or managerial role, that's where!

Another question that will be asked pertains to schooling and whether or not you will be able to apply what you have learned. This is where being prepared really comes into play. Think back on your college courses, especially the ones that correspond to the internship or the job you are seeking. What were the main topics you learned in those courses? Did you do anything to apply those topics to real-world situations? For example, you probably learned about market research in your marketing course, and perhaps you had a project where you actually conducted market research, that is what potential employers want to hear about.

Finally, the last question you will most likely be asked on an interview is if you have any questions for the interviewer. Most students will make the mistake of not asking anything, but don't be fooled. The interviewer wants you to ask some questions. I would limit the questions to 2 or 3, but don't be silly and ask questions about salary, benefits or your first vacation. Ask questions that shows your interest in the company and the job. The best question to ask is, "What happened to the person I will be replacing"? Another question to ask is about how long training is. Lastly, a question about career paths within the organization is a good way to show the interviewer that you are interested in the company and the job.

Remember, do not keep asking a barrage of questions, one after another, to an extent where the interviewer is annoyingly interrupted. For all you know, he may take up the very topics you wanted to ask about during the course of the interview. If, however, you find the interview lagging or dotted with uncomfortable silence, a few well selected questions on your part could bring the interview back on track and at the same time, clear up certain facts important to your understanding of the job, the organization, and how you fit into it. The research you did about the company may help you to formulate a good question.

The next thing to do in order to prepare for the interview is to practice. It may be an old fashioned way, but one way to practice is by answering those questions while you are looking in the mirror. If that is not something you would consider doing then ask a friend or family member to ask you those questions and practice saying your answers out loud. While you are practicing, try to notice any pauses, weird faces, or anything out of the normal when you are practicing your answers out loud. For some of you, this may be the first time you are speaking about any of these topics, and it might take awhile to get comfortable saying it out loud. You need to prepare for and practice for the questions you can anticipate because you might get a question out of left field that might surprise you. Interviewers have been known to ask candidates to compare themselves to a fruit or vegetable. They are probably trying to see how well you perform when thrown a curve.

The night before your interview, lay out the clothes you are going to wear. This may sound weird, but so many things will be racing through your mind the morning of the interview, that it is best to have your clothes ready to go. Make sure that the clothes are professional in nature. Traditional colors of blue and black usually work best. The most important thing to keep in mind is that you are not going to the local club. What that means is, just because you look good in the clothes you wear when you are hanging out with your friends: that does not mean they are appropriate for an interview. In addition, that goes the same for make-up, earrings, nose rings, and any attire out of the ordinary. Be sure your clothing is clean and pressed.

When you get to the interview you have to be prepared to do a few things that will make you stand out. One of the first things you will do is shake hands with the interviewer. There is nothing worse than a sweaty, weak handshake…the "dead fish" handshake. When you are called into the interview, be prepared to shake the interviewer's hand with confidence and a slightly firm grip. Introduce yourself while you are shaking hands and correct any mispronunciation of your name at this time. After this, the interviewer will probably ask you to sit down. Once you sit, the interviewer will ask some of those questions that you have prepared for, but there are some things that you have to do while the interview is going on.

First of all, always use direct eye contact. Never look away when answering questions as it shows lack of interest, or dishonesty. You may be very interested, and telling the truth, but looking away when someone is asking you a question, is a simple body language problem that is misinterpreted by others. Other harmful body language includes fidgeting around in your chair, and moving your hands too much. Sit in your chair with good posture, not too stiff and ridged. Using your hands to express or put an emphasis on something is OK, just try not to do it too often.

Next, use the name of the interviewer when you are responding to questions. Studies have shown that people love to hear their names when they are communicating with others. Not only will your interviewer appreciate hearing his/her name, but he/she will certainly be impressed that you took the care to listen and that you remembered his/her name. It is a small tip that goes a long way.

When the interview is over, make sure you shake hands once again. (No dead fishes!) While you are shaking hands, thank the interviewer for his time and make sure you let the interviewer know how interested you are in getting the job and working for the company. At this point, you can also ask about the company's timeline in choosing an applicant. Asking for a business card as a way of getting in touch with the interviewer is also a good thing to do. Once you get the interviewer's business card, it will be easier for you to send a "thank you letter", because you will have the person's name and address right on the card.

Keep in mind that the interviewer is gauging your reactions to the questions he is asking. In addition, he is looking at your body mannerisms. The following is a brief list of some of the things an interviewer is expecting you to do:

- Interviewee introduced him/herself
- Shook hands in a confident way
- Responded to initial greeting

- Gave relevant response to "tell me about yourself" question
- Knew the position he/she was applying for
- Had an understanding of the nature of the work he/she was applying for
- Answered questions confidently
- Showed interest in the job and career development
- Spoke in a clear way, not using slang
- Thought about questions and answered in complete sentences
- Maintained eye contact throughout the interview
- Did not display negative body language or gestures
- Thanked the interviewer

Thank You Letters

Just as their name implies, thank you letters thank the interviewer for taking time out of his/her day to meet with you. It is strongly suggested to send a "thank you" letter after an interview for a variety of reasons. First of all, you may have forgotten to say something on the interview that you wanted to tell the interviewer. Next, you may want to clarify something that you did say on the interview. You probably really want the internship or the job; by sending a "thank you" letter, you are thanking the interviewer and reminding him/her of why you are the best candidate for the position.

Just like cover letters, thank you letters have a general format as well. The following are common components of a thank you letter:

1. Your contact information
2. The name and address of the Organization, the interviewer's name and title
3. A greeting
4. An opening sentence thanking the interviewer and reminding him/her when you met
5. A few sentences to address points that you forgot to make at the interview
6. A few sentences clarifying points you made at the interview
7. A closing sentence reminding the interviewer that you want the position
8. A formal closing, such as Sincerely
9. Your signature with your name printed underneath

These days thank you notes are often emailed.

Sample Thank You Letter

Your Name
Your Address

Name of Interviewer
Title
Organization Name
Organization's Address

Dear Mr./Mrs. _____:

    Thank you, again, for taking the time to meet with me regarding the marketing internship. It was a pleasure to hear about all of the wonderful things going on at _____ (company name).

    On the interview, I forgot to mention my availability to work on the weekends, should the internship require weekend hours. I also wanted to clarify the level of my Internet research skills. I know that is a valuable asset to have when performing the duties of the internship and I just wanted to assure you that my Internet research skills are more than adequate, and above average.

    I am eager to intern with your organization. Please contact me when you have made your decision. Once again, thank you for taking the time to meet with me.

Sincerely,

Your Signature

Your name typed

Starting Your Internship/Job

Starting a new internship or job can be a very stressful time. You want to be accepted into your new workplace, but you may not know where to begin. The following are a few tips to guide you into settling into your new internship or job.

1. **Get to know your immediate supervisor and co-workers:** Learning the names of the people you are going to work with is the best way to ease into a new position. You will meet many people on your first day on your internship/job, so try to learn the names of the people you will be dealing with most.

2. **Do the small things first:** Simple things like familiarizing yourself to your surroundings is a good way to ease into your new internship/job. Asking where the restrooms are is a good way to start. You would be surprised to find out you might need a key or a code to gain access. In addition, more than likely you will have to fill out human resources paperwork on the first day; so don't be afraid to find out where HR is.

3. **See how the other employees act:** Every company has a culture that is easily identifiable. Listen to how co-workers communicate with each other. Gauge whether the employees are laid back and outgoing, or quiet and reserved. Observe their mannerisms.

4. **Be friendly and smile:** Be friendly and polite and get to know your co-workers. Most people are willing to help out new colleagues and show them the ropes. You would be surprised to see how long a smile goes when meeting new people.

5. **Learn the rules:** Make sure you know the rules of the company. Some companies are very strict with enforcing the rules, whereas others have a more laid back approach. Obviously, make sure you are on time to start work and ready and willing to put in a full shift.

6. **Learn the customs:** Every internship/job workplace has customs associated with it. Things like bringing your lunch to work, or eating lunch inside the office is something worthwhile noting. In addition, if staying late is something that everyone does, you may want to join in.

7. **Take note of how employees dress:** It is important to know the dress code at your workplace. Whether you are a new employee or an intern, you have to note how the other employees are dressed as it is up to you to conform to the dress code.

8. **Familiarize yourself with your duties and responsibilities:** If you are starting a new job, most companies will provide you with some sort of training program. If you are an intern, it is up to you to make sure you know what is expected of you. Some companies will have you actively participating right at the beginning, whereas other companies will allow you to sit with an existing employee and see the duties he performs. This practice is known as job shadowing.

9. **Do not be afraid to ask questions:** Ask questions, especially when it is related to your job duties and responsibilities. After you know what is expected of you, and you start to perform some of the job duties, you want to make sure that what you are doing is correct.

If you are an intern, it is expected that you will ask questions because you are there to learn. Always ask questions if you are unsure of anything.

10. **Be proactive**: If you are starting a new job, see if there is any additional work you can do to help the organization. Don't get me wrong; do not try to do everything just to please your boss because your co-workers will misinterpret your actions as being phony. If you are an intern, start to seek out additional responsibilities, once you have mastered the initial tasks. In both cases, this shows initiative and will go a long way with your new supervisor and co-workers.

If you engage in the above activities, then your transition into your new internship/job will be a lot smoother. Co-workers will like the fact that you are trying to fit in, and supervisors will like that you are showing initiative in learning and succeeding in your new internship/job. There may be times in the beginning where everything will be overwhelming and you will want to quit, but if you stick with it, and utilize some of these tips, you will be successful.

For more information on specific grading criteria, please look through the Intern Rating Sheet at the end of the workbook.

Communication

In order to have effective communication with someone, you should think, before you speak. To have positive communication, you have to practice saying things in an acceptable way, in a professional manner, without using slang. Most, if not all of you, will be working in an office environment, as part of a team effort to produce results. Interpersonal communication is vital to this effort. Be careful about using slang that might be understood by you and your friends but might be misinterpreted by others. Each of the following examples may create communication barriers because they can cause offense. Rewrite each in such a way that it would be appropriate in an office setting.

Poor Communication	Better Communication
What up?	
A'ight	
What a dumb idea!	
Don't call me girl/boy!	
What d'ya want me doin?	
Are you stupid or something?	
Why don't you teach me something?	
This job is dumb!	
Get outta my face, yo!	
I quit, idiot!	

Communication between you and your co-workers, supervisors, and most importantly, your customers is important. When dealing with customers, you must maintain a positive attitude, and listen to what the needs of the customer are. When you understand the situation, you can then make a better decision when answering customers.

Get involved in your internship so when you are approached, you will know how to respond to customers. Know what you can and cannot do. If you are empowered to deal with customers, be as professional as you can. If there is something with which you are unfamiliar, do not hesitate to ask a co-worker, your internship supervisor or immediate manager. If all else fails, do not be afraid to say: "I'm sorry, but I am an intern and I am learning the job".

Categories of on the Job Performance

When you are on your internship, your performance will be evaluated in a variety of areas. The following is a brief list of criteria on which you will be evaluated: productivity, quality of work, relationship with clientele, communication, writing ability, responsibility, independent functioning, attendance and punctuality, attitude toward learning, judgment, application skills, problem solving skills, etc.

When you are performing the duties and responsibilities on your internship, take the time to write about how you feel you performed using the above criteria. Answer and explain your responses to these questions:

1. The duties of the job were?

2. Did I do a lot/a little work?

3. Did I do a good/poor job?

4. How did I interact with customers?

5. How did I communicate with co-workers, supervisors, customers?

6. Was I responsible?

7. Was I a team player?

8. Did I always need help?

9. Was I able to work alone?

10. Did I solve any problems?

11. Did I always show up when I was supposed to?

12. Was I on-time every day, including when I returned from lunch or breaks?

13. How was my attitude?

14. Is there a link between my academic training and my professional goals?

15. Was my writing good? (Includes course work)

If you can answer the above questions in a positive manner, then you are probably going to get a good grade in the course!

Perception

In attempting to improve our understanding of human behavior, we should develop the habit of looking for numerous causes, not THE cause, of any given behavior. We should also assume that the way something appears to us may well not be the way it looks to others. From previous studies on personal and group perception and motivation, 5 principles stand out as being particularly important in exploring behavioral patterns:

1. **The way a person behaves depends on both the person and his/her environment**. It is thus important to give attention to the individual, the situation and the relation between the individual and the situation. To change behavior, change the person, either through education or training, or change the situation, through procedures, rules, etc.

2. **Each individual behaves in ways which make sense to him/her**. For example, you are working at the front desk of a hotel and you have to tell a client that his reservation was cancelled because he came in late. The person gets very upset and starts to rant and rave. You must NOT take this personally. The client is acting that way because he learned it from another person or role model, or he believes that acting that way will bring him the results he desires.

3. **An individual's perception of the situation influences his/her behavior in the situation.** Our picture of reality is influenced by previous experiences. We develop systematic points of view. If a person fails at something, they may perceive themselves as a failure in other situations as well.

4. **An individual's view of him/herself influences what he/she does.** If someone thinks he is a tough guy, then he will act aggressively in most situations. If a person is shy, then he will most likely keep to him/herself and not wish to communicate with others.

5. **An individual's behavior is influenced by his needs, which vary between people and from time to time.** Sometimes people are in a hurry and want things done immediately and they do not take other people's situations into consideration. Also, sometimes people act differently in front of a boss or someone of influence.

Our perception comes into play all the time, whether we are choosing a job, a mate, significant other, or an internship. What one student may perceive as the ultimate internship may be a horrible experience to someone else. For example, an internship in a housekeeping department may look terrible to some students, but it may look like an opportunity to learn a great deal about budgets, people and leadership to others.

Look at the above principles. I am sure you have seen them applied in the real world already, and if you haven't, I am sure that you definitely will see them applied throughout your career, and maybe even throughout your internship. You have probably heard the term, "You can take the guy out of Brooklyn, but you can't take the Brooklyn out of the guy". That is someone's perception speaking. Everyone is going to make a snap opinion of someone they just meet; it's human nature, it's perception.

You have probably also heard people say, "Oh that person is no good, he's from _____" (fill in the blank with the local bad neighborhood.) Sometime's people make a character decision based on the neighborhood someone is from. Think about it, what would your immediate perception be about a person you just met who told you that he lived in the local bad neighborhood? Again, that perception is wrong, but it is a way of life.

Unfortunately a person's beliefs of him/herself often interfere with one's perceptions as well. A person can sometimes think he is _____. Fill in the blank with a variety of words such as: smart, funny, stupid, dumb, ugly, handsome, rich, etc. Problems arise when the person starts to believe they are these things to the extreme. If someone believes that he is dumb, then that will interfere with his perception of whether he will be able to accomplish his goals. The same thing goes for the person who is too overconfident and finds that he is also unable to achieve his goals because he thinks things will come easy to him and not work for it.

In this age of the Internet, students should also be wary about what they post about themselves on social networking web sites, or video web sites such as youtube.com. It is not unheard of for employers to Google the name of an internship/job applicant only to find some incriminating behavior about the applicant that leads the company to decide not to hire the applicant. You may have posted a video of yourself where you were having fun, but the perception of the employer, after watching the video, leads him/her to think that you are unsuited for a position in the company.

Finally, humans are a funny breed. The co-worker with whom you have a great time laughing and joking around might also be the person reporting all of your wrong doings to your boss just to get ahead in the company. You will find that some people in the workplace are only out for themselves and they perceive that being a whistleblower is the way to move up in an organization. People have a tendency not to act the same way they act with co-workers as they do when the boss is around.

Problems on Your Internship

Although no one expects interns to have difficulties on their internship, sometimes problems do arise. When issues arise, it is important for the intern to realize that the problems can be worked out. Small problems, like not being able to make a shift due to a school conflict are easy; just call in advance and tell your internship supervisor about the situation. Always communicate with your internship supervisor in order to maximize your participation throughout the internship.

Larger problems are rare and varied. However, interns must realize that there are consequences associated with serious problems that arise on the internship that reach far beyond receiving a failing grade in the course. Listed below are some common problems found on the internship and some ideas of how to deal with them.

1. **The internship is not what the intern expected**: On occasion, internships are not what the intern expected. Sometimes it is because students thought the work would be different. Other times, it is the realization that the actual work is something that the intern does not want to do in the future. If that is the case, then the internship has provided the intern with valuable information to make a better career choice. If the internship is not what you expected, and you cannot work out through the problems, contact your faculty supervisor immediately.

2. **The duties/responsibilities are boring**: All internships are not created equally. Some internship providers will allow interns to perform hands-on work, whereas other internships might just allow the intern to shadow an employee. Interns take internships to get a better understanding of the how their chosen industry works; interns are not the President of the company. Therefore, soak up as much information as possible. If interns would like to do more hands-on work, then they should be proactive, and ask their internship supervisors if this is possible. If it is not possible to take on more duties and responsibilities, then experience and learn as much as possible about your industry.

3. **Time commitment**: One of the biggest problems with interns is underestimating the time commitment to the internship. Today's students have a variety of time constraints. Most students have full-time school schedules, and a part-time job, not to mention family and personal time commitments. It is difficult to schedule in some time for your internship. If time is a factor, put off your internship until you can actually do the internship hours without a problem. If after you have already started your internship, time becomes a problem, contact your faculty advisor for suggestions. Do not just stop going to the internship!

4. **Personality Conflicts**: Sometimes the intern does not like the internship provider, and the internship provider does not like the intern. Although this rarely happens, the intern should not be rude at any time. If personality conflicts become too much to deal with,

contact your faculty supervisor immediately. Your faculty supervisor will act as a liaison between you and your internship supervisor, so utilize your faculty supervisor as needed. Internship providers will contact the faculty supervisor if there is a problem as well, so it works both ways.

5. **Interns just stop going to the internship**: I cannot tell you how many times this has happened over the years. For some reasons, interns just stop going to the internship for a variety of reasons. The problem is, the interns do not tell anyone! If you are having a problem on your internship, let your faculty supervisor know **immediately**. Your faculty supervisor will intervene on your behalf. Again, do not just stop going to the internship.

6. **Intern not performing well**: Sometimes, an internship supervisor will contact your faculty supervisor to say that the intern is not performing well. If this happens, your faculty supervisor will meet with you to discuss what he/she was advised. More than likely, you will be asked not to return to the internship. Although this is a bad situation, the good part is that the intern will not have to deal with the internship provider directly.

These are just a few problems that may arise on the internship. Other problems may arise when you are on your internship that have not been mentioned above. If this occurs, contact your faculty advisor as soon as possible. Do not just stop going to your internship. Interns, especially ones that were placed by faculty supervisors, have to realize that the internship locations are usually long-term relationships that your faculty supervisor has established throughout the years. If you stop going to an internship, or perform badly, you are ruining established relationships, and may even prevent future interns from being placed at the internship location.

There have been various internship problems over the course of the years. Simple problems have arisen where personal issues interfered with the internship commitment, and the intern just stopped going to the internship. Serious problems have arisen where interns have threatened internship supervisors to give good grades or they would cause problems. In both instances, the students failed the course, but more importantly, the internship location refused to take future interns.

Always remember, that your faculty advisor is your liaison between you and your internship supervisor. Utilize your faculty advisor whenever the slightest problem arises, or whenever you think a problem will arise.

Self-efficacy

Albert Bandura defined self-efficacy as people's beliefs about their capabilities to produce effects. When contemplating your career, you should take the time to think about how you believe how well prepared you are to perform in a certain job. Some people do this by taking an inventory of the skills they have accumulated throughout their career. However, just because you have gained a skill, that does not necessarily mean you believe you can perform a certain task. Only you know yourself better than anyone.

Think back on your internship. What did you like? What did you do well? Also think about the duties and responsibilities of the job you are looking to acquire. When you are finished, answer the following questions by putting a checkmark next to your self-efficacy in the topic:

____   I like to work alone.

____   I like to work with other people.

____   I like to be in charge.

____   I like to follow the boss.

____   I like to take on responsibility in the workplace.

____   I am happy to let others take responsibility in the workplace.

____   I like to work in a busy place.

____   I need quiet to work best.

____   I like to work with my head.

____   I like to work with my hands and create things.

____   I like to be active.

____   I like to be still.

____   I like to make good money even if I do not like the job.

____   I need to change from task to task and day to day.

____   I like to follow the same routine every day.

____   I like to work early hours.

____   I like to work late.

Values

Core values are a system of beliefs that are basic to the character of each individual. You make all of your decisions based upon the values you, yourself, have come to accept. People value things in different ways and at different times in their lives. People also value things differently in their personal and professional lives. What may be important to you at home, may not necessarily be important to you at work.

As you are growing up, your parents introduce you to their ideas. Certain concepts you hold may have come from religious training. At every phase of your life, your friends can affect convictions through peer pressure. You must remember, though, that ultimately your choices are your own responsibility. As an adult, no one can be held accountable for your actions except yourself with your own value system.

When you were young, you probably were influenced by your parents the most. You saw your mother and father working hard to provide for you. They probably took you to church and taught you the difference between right and wrong. They may have even taught you the value of money, or that nothing takes the place of family. Whatever it was, you held those values high because of the influence your family had on you.

As you got older, you started to experience new things. You started to hang around with different people. Maybe you met some friends through participation in sports, or through other after-school activities. You probably started to become friends with more people that had the same common interests as you did. Your values probably revolved around hanging out and having fun. However, as you get older, your values still continue to change. Now you are in college, and have placed a higher value on getting an education. Eventually, you will start your own families, if you haven't done so already, and find that education will take a back seat to raising your children.

Each and every culture offers its own special influences. For example, in some Latin American countries, workers go home for a three-hour break, or "siesta", every afternoon. The siesta is a preferred, or "valued", way of life. If a worker in the United States were to go home in the afternoon for three hours, he would probably lose his job! The siesta is a chosen value for a relaxed pace of life in those Latin American countries. In the U.S., workers are urged to do the most work in the shortest amount of time to make as much money as possible. It would seem that in this country the value of money is more important than a relaxed way of life.

Problems with values arise when you work with someone that does not share the same values that you do. You can choose your friends, but you cannot choose your co-workers, so learning how to deal with someone that does not have the same values as yourself is very important. Some people look at their jobs as just a way to put money in their pockets. They are not worried about being promoted. All they care about is that weekly paycheck. Others may value being promoted and will do anything to move ahead. Staying late, pleasing the boss, doing whatever it takes at the risk of not having a personal life, might be more appealing to some people.

Bear in mind that having these values are not a matter of right or wrong. It is simply a matter of what someone believes is more important, and that is why your values might change as time goes on and situations change. What was important to you when you were younger may not be as important to you now. Values can, and will, change as you widen your horizons. The intent of this lesson is to make you aware of the values you have now and may acquire in the future, so that you will be true to yourself when making the important decisions in your life.

List the top five things you value most in your life:

1. _____
2. _____
3. _____
4. _____
5. _____

Now list the top five things you value in an internship/job.

1. _____
2. _____
3. _____
4. _____
5. _____

Are they different? Do they conflict? Do you see yourself changing your values in the next 5 years?

Career Decision Making

There are many important decisions you will make throughout your life about your career. Where will you work? Why type of work will you do? Where will you get the necessary skills to go into a certain industry? You have already started to make some of those decisions by going to this school and studying within your major. When making career decisions, oftentimes, people make decisions based on what they value, whereas other people make decisions based purely on money. However, you decide on what you ultimately do, you need to gather enough information in order to make the best decision possible. Some people make up a pro/con list for each alternative.

Gathering information is the most important element in making decisions. This is so, because any decision involves risk-taking. Whatever you do, it will be different from what would have happened had you decided to elect one of the other alternatives. Perhaps the outcome of the decision you made is not all you wished for; another alternative might have given you more satisfaction. That risk is always present. The best thing to do is to decide on the alternative that seems best after studying all the possibilities then accept the result of your decision. You might say to yourself, "You win a few, and you lose a few."

In decision making, there are six (6) critical questions

1. What is the decision to be made? This could be something like choosing one company over another to work at.

2. What is important to me about this decision? Is it the hours, the salary, etc.?

3. What do I need to know to make a good decision? What is important to me?

4. What do I already know that will help? Do I have all of the accurate information from the interview?

5. What more do I need to know? Did I cover all of my bases?

6. Where can I get the missing information? Can I call human resources, or maybe someone that works at the company?

After you have finished working through the six parts of decision making, then you have gathered enough information to make a better decision. One of the first career decisions you are going to have to make concerns your internship. Did you like the work? Are you happy doing the type of work involved in your chosen industry? Is this an industry you can grow in? Can you earn a living wage? These are just some of the career decisions you will make throughout your lifetime.

Barriers to Career Exploration

Barriers to career exploration occur for a variety of reasons. Oftentimes, it is because the job seeker did not do enough research about a particular career. It is like someone wanting to be a surgeon and not being able to handle the sight of blood! Usually people hear, or see about a job that appeals to them in some way and then immediately say, "I want to do that". Hardly anyone takes the time to research a career to find out all about the little details involved. Figuring out your career path is hard work but, it's worth it!

In addition to not being informed about a particular career, there are a variety of other barriers to career exploration that include both internal and external factors. Internal barriers include: anxiety with making a career choice, concern about multiple responsibilities, unwillingness to do the required work, procrastination, etc. External barriers include: the economy, educational requirements, employment outlook, etc.

Hopefully, your internship and some of the exercises you did in this workbook have relieved some of your anxiety about choosing a career. Becoming more pro-active in learning more about the duties and responsibilities of a particular job should help alleviate your anxiety. In addition, everyone has to learn good time management skills and acquire the ability to multi-task and handle multiple responsibilities. It seems that the new generation of workers are able to do that increasingly better than the previous generation of workers has.

Major external barriers like a bad economy and not being able to afford the educational requirements of a certain job, are a lot more difficult to deal with. However, this does not mean you should throw in the towel and give up. These obstacles simply mean that you must work harder to achieve your goals. For example, sending out more resumes and working harder to find a job in a bad economy, and going out and getting a student loan when more education is required to advance in a certain profession.

Identify 3 internal barriers to your career exploration.

1.

2.

3.

Identify 3 external barriers to your career exploration.

1.

2.

3.

Career Planning

Students do not often see the big picture of planning for their careers. Granted, that may be for a variety of things including age and lack of experience. However, career planning is very important.

Career goal mapping can be done for the short-term as well as the long-term. You must start by doing a variety of the things you have done for this course, starting with tentatively selecting a career field that best matches your personal skills and interests. You must then consider the education and training requirements for the chosen career, experience requirements, employment outlook and the economy, etc.

Throughout this workbook, you have learned about the importance of information gathering and putting yourself into a position to make a better career decision. Most of the assignments that you have done will help you to plan your future career. Researching a career is very important in order to plan your career. For example, if you want to be a lawyer, obviously you have to go to law school, but before that can happen, you have to take the LSAT.

Knowing what the requirements are for a certain career is very important. If there is an educational requirement, it is up to you to find out what that is. If there are experiential requirements, it is up to you to find out how long it is and how you can go about acquiring the experience. You need a plan to guide you from where you are now to where you eventually wish to be. You are in school now, but what's next? A job? More schooling? What is the best path for you to take to get to your dream job?

What are 5 skills or traits you need to know about the career you wish to obtain, and what are you going to do in order to obtain those skills or traits?

1.

2.

3.

4.

5.

Assignments

Resume Assignment

A resume is an advertisement of yourself. Your resume's primary objective is to gain the attention and interest of a prospective employer about you and your qualifications for the job. Your resume must have contact information, as well as detailed data about your work history, education, and skill set. If you make a grammatical or spelling error on your resume, you can pretty much kiss your chances of being asked in for an interview goodbye.

There are many styles or formats in which a resume can be presented. None are right or wrong - it is a matter of your personal preference of a particular style. The first part of this assignment is to make sure you have read through the resume writing section of this workbook. Next, do an internet search for "resume samples" and search through the various samples that are on the internet. Most colleges should have a career development office. Visit your school's career office and pick up any material that they distribute on resume formats and preparation. Review the materials and select a format that suits you.

Some students elect to use a template from a popular software program. If you decide to do this make sure you are comfortable with the style and format. In my experience, most templates are not suitable because the contact information is too small. At the very least if you decide to use a template be prepared to make some changes to the format.

Regardless of the resume style chosen, there are some rules that you must pay heed to:

1 - Never lie. Tell the truth, but select those truths that are most appealing and interesting about you.

2 - Resumes are prepared in reverse chronological order. Your most recent accomplishment is listed FIRST.

3 - Resumes must be visually pleasing. They must look nice, with the type spread over the page and not bunched up in a corner. Resumes must be typed - with no errors. A resume must be letter perfect. Use resume-quality paper.

Your assignment is, to select a format and word process your resume. In addition you are to make your resume "electronic". Electronic resumes allow different word processors to read your file. In order to make your resume electronic, you must click on "Save As". A save as window will appear. In the bottom of the window, you can name your file and right underneath that you have a "save as type" choice. Click on the down arrow and choose Rich Text Format, and then click on save. Your resume is now electronic and you should use this version when emailing your resume.

When you are finished, email your resume to your professor. Make sure it is in rich text format.

Internship/Job Search Assignment

As you learned, the Internet is a powerful tool that you can utilize to make your internship/job search easier. What makes the Internet so powerful is the access the user gets to millions and millions of web pages throughout the world. These web pages make information easily obtainable, just by entering some information and clicking your mouse.

In order to search the Internet, you need a web browser with a powerful search engine. A search engine allows your computer to search through all of those millions of web pages and provide you with results that best matches whatever it is you are looking for. Some common search engines are Google.com, and Yahoo.com.

All search engines have a search field, a box that you can type in the information you are looking for. You can enter as many words as you want, just a few, or sometimes entire sentences. Either way, the search engine will give you back a listing of the web sites that match whatever it is you are searching for. For example, if you were looking for web sites or information about Jobs, you would type "jobs" in the search box and then hit enter.

The results you obtain will be a list of web sites that contain the word "jobs" in it. Since jobs is such a broad topic, you will probably receive millions and millions of results. I don't think you have time to go through a million web sites, so it is advantageous to be more specific. A better search term would be "jobs in marketing" or whatever employment area you are looking for. Additionally, a search using "jobs in marketing in NYC" will narrow down your results even more. You can use the same searches for internships, just change the search term to internship as opposed to job. For example type: "internships in NYC" in the search field.

A word of caution: companies pay to have their results appear to the top of the results list. These web sites tend to be sites that you have to pay to use, so proceed to them with caution. Also, there are thousands of unscrupulous businesses on the Internet, so when you go to any of the results, make sure you go in cautiously.

For this assignment, go to a search engine of your choice and type in the search terms below. Write out any interesting web sites that provided you with good information.

Search Term	**Interesting Web Sites**
1. Internships	_____
2. Business internships	_____
3. Internships in NYC	_____
4. Business internships in NYC	_____
5. Hotel internships NYC	_____
6. Jobs	_____
7. Jobs in NYC	_____
8. Marketing Jobs in NYC	_____
9. Hotel Jobs in NYC	_____
10. The name of a specific company you want to work for	_____

Online Employment Databases Assignment

There are many different types of employment databases on the Internet. You may have heard of the more popular companies like careerbuilder.com, and monster.com that frequently advertise on television and radio. We have also learned that The New York Times has partnered with Monster.com to administer its employment classified advertisements. These companies are just a few of the employment databases on the Internet.

You may have found other employment databases. For many Hospitality students, I suggest that they join www.hcareers.com. Even though these web sites primarily offer jobs, they also list internships from time to time as well. Additionally, there are also web sites that specifically cater to students looking for internships as well. Web sites such as www.internships.com and www.internjobs.com are just a few that specialize in internships. These companies have web sites that maintain databases to internship/employment classified advertisements throughout the Unites States, as well as international locations. Most of their services are free to the user. However, they usually require you to register to access their databases.

Beware! While the Internet is a valuable tool for finding an internship/job, there are some unscrupulous companies that prey on unsuspecting people. Some companies have very elaborate web sites and ask you to become a member, just like the companies above do. However, these unscrupulous companies will promise you everything and ask you for a credit card number to insure that you will get their "valuable information" and a "dream job". These web sites will take your money and provide you with information that you can find on your own, for free. A good rule to follow is: if the offer is too good to be true, then it probably is. Use caution.

For this assignment you must register for the services of 2 online employment database companies. You can either use any of the web sites listed above, or any that you find on your own, or any combination of the two.

To do this, you need to go to the web site and find the link that enables you to register. After you click on that link, you will see an application that asks you to fill-in various personal information. You need to fill out the application to the best of your ability. The more accurate your information in, the better the web site will be able to match you to the internships/jobs in the database. You will need a valid email address in order for you to receive emails from them that match your skills with the internship/job postings that come into the web site.

Print out or copy and paste the confirmation page after you have registered. Email the file to your professor when you are done. Remember, you need two of them!

Resume Posting on the Internet

After you have registered at one of the online employment database web sites you will be able to access their databases and be able to post your resume online. Posting your resume online is a good idea if you want to constantly be considered for jobs. After your resume is posted, it will constantly be matched up to all new job offerings the company receives. When the company matches your resume to a job listing, they will send you an email to review the job posting. It is then up to you to review the job offering and email your resume to the company looking to hire.

To Search the Database:

When you go to the web site of the employment database you joined, there should be a link to "Search Jobs". After you click on that link, a page will come up and ask you to provide more information. Depending on the individual web site, it might provide a search box and ask you to list a specific industry or position, or the site may have a menu for you to choose a desired industry. You can be specific as "airline customer service" or as general as "airlines". Either way, you will be given the results that match the jobs already posted on the online employment database.

Posting Your Resume:

When you visit the web site there will be a link for you to "post your resume". After clicking on the link, follow the instructions to post your resume. Some sites make it very easy, and all you will need to do is copy and paste your resume from an existing file. Other sites may require you to change your resume into an electronic resume. Don't Fear! See the Resume Assignment in this workbook to learn how to make your resume "electronic".

Remember, electronic resumes enable employers to scan your resumes for key words. Key words are specific skills or requirements that must be contained in your resume in order to be considered for the position.

Part #1: Do some research on an online agency's database. Find 3 jobs/internships that you would want, and print out the job postings for all. Circle the keywords in the job posting that you believe the employer wishes to see on your resume.

Part #2: Post your resume with the 2 agencies that you registered with and print out the page that confirms that your resume has been posted.

Job Application Worksheet

General Information

Name (Last)	First	Middle Initial	Home Telephone Number ( )
Address (Street)	City	State	Zip	Other Telephone Number ( )
E-mail address	Are you legally able to work in the United States? Yes No		

Position Information

Name of Position you are applying for	Type: Full time Temporary Part time Internship
Do you have any physical, mental or medical impairment which would prevent you from performing the activities involved in the job for which you are applying? Yes____ No____	Shift: Day Evening Overnight Rotating Other
Salary Desired	Date Available

Education

Name and location of school	Dates attended: Month/Year	Graduate? Yes or No?	Degree Type	Major

List any special Skills or training you have:

_____

_____

Work Experience

Name/ Location of Business	Dates Employed	Job Title	Description of Duties	Reason for leaving

May we contact your previous employers?   Yes   No

Personal References: please list the contact information for 3 personal references that are not family members.

Name	Address	Telephone Number

I certify that the above information is accurate, correct and complete. I understand that if hired, any false information contained on this application may be sufficient cause for dismissal.

Signature of Applicant_____   **Date** _____

Interview Questions Assignment

A job interview is like theatre. You are like an actor in a play who must come prepared to be in a musical or a drama, without knowing the lines of the script. The only way to succeed is learning to think quickly, respond firmly, and not be afraid to take positions and make statements.

Your assignment is to answer the following list of frequently asked interview questions. Answer all of the questions to the best of your ability, in 2 to 3 sentences.

1) Tell me about yourself.
2) Why should I hire you for this position?
3) What is your best quality?
4) What can we expect from you if you are hired?
5) What is your biggest accomplishment?
6) What would you consider to be your greatest weakness?
7) What things do you look for in an organization?
8) What areas do you think you can improve upon?
9) Do you prefer to work in groups or alone?
10) What type of people do you find the most difficult to work with?
11) Where do you see yourself in five years?
12) What did you like most about your last job?
13) What did you like least about your last job?
14) How has school prepared you for work?
15) This job requires leadership skills or organizational skills. What in your experience shows that you have skills in this area?
16) Do you have any questions for me?

Perception Assignment

Perception, or how we see things, is unique to each individual. As children, we have all played the party game of "Telephone", where a person initiates a message and passes it along through a chain of people, to the final receiver, who must repeat the message. Invariably, the message that comes out at the end is very different from the one at the beginning.

In similar fashion, two people perceiving the same object or describing the perception of the same room, will vary greatly in their description because of their subjective values and how they interpret the importance, style, color, texture, etc. of the objects in the room.

How we perceive other people is even more complex. Each person is a unique blend of physical, intellectual and emotional characteristics many of which are hidden below the surface. How many people do you know who claim to be different than they appear to be on the surface?

As difficult a chore as perceiving others turns out to be, how we perceive ourselves, or see ourselves is even more difficult. We may turn a particular face to the outside world so that we are perceived in a particular fashion, but how about inside? How about our private selves? Is how others see us the same as how we see ourselves, or is it different?

For this assignment, you are required to type two (2), 1 page essays, single spaced, or 2 page essays, double spaced: The topic of the first essay is, "How Others See Me," the topic of the 2nd essay is, "How I See Myself."

Word process both of your essays and email them to your professor when you are finished. Be sure that both submissions are error free or someone might perceive you in a negative fashion!

Perception Assignment #2

Your assignment is to paint a word portrait of yourself. Select 15 terms listed below that best describes you. Type a short paragraph (4-5 sentences) about EACH term that explains why that term describes you. Give an example from your personal experience in each paragraph.

Submissive, procrastinator, different, snob, professional, giving, selfish, loving, calm, strong, patient, logical, quiet, serious, shy, flaky, friendly, honest, nice, sincere, worrier, insecure, survivor, impatient, hard working, conceited, knowledgeable, self-conscious, orderly, nervous, positive, sarcastic, creative, short-tempered, innovative, sense of humor, adaptable, giving, sensitive, caring, outgoing, stubborn, open-minded, generous, intelligent, self-critical, strong-minded, respectful, compassionate, timid, insecure, enthusiastic, achiever, religious, make snap judgments, lazy, impatient, aggressive, ambitious, docile

Word process your assignment and email it to your professor when you are finished.

Self-efficacy Assignment

Self-efficacy is one's confidence in his ability to accomplish a specific task. There are many things that an employer expects of an employee right from the start. Soft skills, like communicating and dressing properly are a given by today's employers, however, most jobs require certain skills that you should have been exposed to, and learned, through your academic experiences.

For this assignment, please rate your self-efficacy as to how it relates to the ideal job that you wish to have in the future. If you already have your ideal job, relate whether you were really prepared from the beginning, or the things you did to acclimate yourself to your job when you first started. Make sure you give yourself a rating and justify it.

Write a 1 page essay, single spaced, or 2 page essay, double spaced, paper.
Word process your assignment and email it to your professor when you are finished.

Values Assignment

A person's values illuminate his/hers life. When thinking about values in an abstract sense, it is easy to know what is right. However, when making a career decision, sometimes things are not so simple and clear.

The following situation presents a typical problem in career values. You are answering the question posed in the last paragraph with a 500 word essay that explains your choice.

When it comes to his career, Sam deals in only one currency, and that is money. Sam wants "big bucks" and he wants them fast. Human relations and compassion (other forms of exchange) have no appeal to Sam. You can read Sam's attitude in his movements. He appears totally confident and he seems to know when to be aggressive at just the right time. As a result, many of his classmates envy him for the job opportunities that he is bound to have offered to him.

Ralph is a quiet dissenter. Ralph feels that money is important but that it comes to those who select careers that contribute to the lives of others as much as to those who take a direct mega-bucks approach. Ralph made this comment to Sam (a good friend of his) yesterday: "You're going to make it fast Sam, but I think I will be happier getting to where I'm going. And, who knows, I might wind up with as much money as you while my personal values remain intact. I think you are sacrificing human-relation values for the dollar, and in life, this is not necessary".

Sam replied: "It's a jungle out there Ralph. You may wind up as happy as I do. But, you and your values will get pushed around so much that you will be sidelined as far as money is concerned. I can worry about values after I have it made".

How would you reply if you were part of the above conversation? Would you side with Sam or Ralph? How do you intend to maintain your personal values and still enjoy monetary success?

Write a 1 page essay, single spaced, or 2 page essay, double spaced with your responses. Word process your assignment and email it to your professor when you are finished.

Decision-Making Assignment

For this assignment, please make sure you have read through the Career Decision Making section of this workbook. When you are finished, write a 1 page essay single spaced, or 2 page essay double spaced relating to a career-oriented decision that you are in the process of making or will make in the future.

Your essay should:
a) identify the decision,
b) list all of the alternatives or choices of action that are possible,
c) outline all of the reasons for and against each possible alternative or choice,
d) gauge the risk involved in each alternative or choice, and finally,
e) indicate the way you have chosen to go.

Remember, a decision-making strategy is a way to clarify your thinking about reaching a goal by the best possible route as you see it.

You win a few and lose a few, but keep on trying. Each time you try to make a sound decision, you develop more skill in the process.

Word process your assignment and email it to your professor when you are finished.

Workplace Personality Assignment

Your personality goes a long way in determining how well you will fit in with a certain organization. Different organizations have different management styles, and your personality plays a substantial part in how well you will work within different corporate structures. While everyone says that they are the best employee, never late, open to criticism, etc., only you know your true personality and how good of an employee you really are.

One of the ways to determine your workplace personality is to take a test that gives you a score of how well you will do within different types of corporate structures. There are a variety of tests on the web that will allow you to do this, free of charge. Please take the test located at: http://www.humanmetrics.com/cgi-win/JTypes2.asp and have your work personality scored. YOU WILL NOT BE GRADED ON THIS ASSIGNMENT SO BE AS TRUTHFUL AS POSSIBLE WHEN TAKING THE TEST.

After you take the test and score it, review your results. What type of work personality do you have? Do you agree or disagree with the results? Write a 1 page essay, single-spaced, or 2 page, double-spaced, paper that discusses the test and the results. Discuss whether or not you agree with the results and why?

Word process your assignment and email it to your professor when you are finished.

Corporate Culture Assignment

Corporations have been defined as "artificial persons". Just like each individual, every corporation has a personality. When looking for a job, it is important to match the personality of the individual with the personality of the corporation to assure the happiest result for each. To assist you in making this decision, three basic corporate personality types are defined below:

THEORY X - Is the traditional managerial assumption that employees dislike work and must be controlled to motivate them to work toward the achievement of organizational objectives. Motivation comes from the organization because that's how the employees want it.

THEORY Y - Assumes that, under proper conditions, workers accept and seek out responsibilities in order to fulfill their self-actualization (social esteem) needs. Theory Y states that work is as natural as play or rest and that motivation comes from within the individual.

THEORY Z - Is the assumption that organizations develop their own culture, combining the organization and the employee into a community, where since everyone knows what is correct behavior everyone does what is expected of them. Motivation grows out of this combined culture.

Carefully examine these three statements and select the type of organizational personality (X, Y or Z) that you would be most comfortable with.

Your assignment is to write a 1 page essay, single spaced, or 2 page essay, double spaced, explaining your choice of organizational personality and why it fits your needs and objectives.

Word process your assignment and email it to your professor when you are finished.

Managerial Style Assignment

Assume that you are the owner/manager of a small business. (Try to make it a business within your academic discipline). Write a 1 page single spaced or 2 page double spaced essay, always giving your reasons for each choice, describing the following:

1 - The type of organization you would run (X,Y or Z).

2 - Your values in handling employees.

3 - The type of management style you would adopt as owner/manager. (Authoritarian, democratic or laissez-faire (hands off).

4 - Does your management style as owner/manager differ from the treatment that you would expect as an employee?

Write a 1 page essay, single spaced, or 2 page essay, double spaced, with your answers. Word process your assignment and email it to your professor when you are finished.

Career Research Assignment

Students should take the time to find out more about the careers they wish to go into. There are a variety of ways one can go about finding out about careers, the easiest way is to use the Occupational Outlook Handbook. You can get to the OOH through the www.bls.gov/ooh web site.

Look through the OOH and write a small research paper that describes what you find with regard to the career you would like to have in the future. How much is the salary? Is there job growth? What are the trends? etc.

Write a 1 page essay, single spaced, or 2 page essay, double spaced, with your results.

Word process your assignment and email it to your professor when you are finished.

Specialization Assignment

The term business is a general term that encompasses a variety of different industries. To say you want to work in business is like saying you want to make money. Everyone wants to make money, but there are a variety of ways to achieve that goal. More than likely, if you are getting a degree in business, you have studied a variety of different subject areas in order to obtain the tools commonly found in business organizations. Some of those subjects are: accounting, marketing, human resources, finance, management, operations, law, and logistics, just to name a few. While knowing a little about all of those different areas is great, most employers like to see a specialization in one specific area. How do you know which area is right for you?

If you took all of your courses already you probably liked one subject area over another, no matter what the reason is. However, in order to be successful in your internship you need to be able to explain WHY you chose one area to specialize in. Employers will probably ask you this type of question on an interview. So how do you answer that question?

Review your notes from the business courses you have taken, especially the notes from the course in the subject area in which you hope to specialize. What makes that subject matter interesting to you? Why do you think you want to specialize in that area? What makes it different from other courses and other subject matter? What makes you think that you will be able to work, succeed and advance in this area? What makes you think that working in this subject area will excite you and bring you into work happy every day?

After considering all of those questions, and a few of your own, please write a 1 page essay, single spaced, or 2 page essay, double spaced, outlining the reasons why you want to work in ...(your subject area).

Word process your assignment and email it to your professor when you are finished.

Barriers to Career Exploration Assignment

There are a variety of barriers to career exploration including both internal and external factors. Internal barriers include: anxiety with making a career choice, concern about multiple responsibilities, procrastination, laziness, etc. External barriers include: the economy, educational requirements, employment outlook, etc.

For this assignment, 1 page essay, single spaced, or 2 page essay, double spaced paper about all of the barriers to career exploration you have encountered and how you plan on overcoming them.

Word process your assignment and email it to your professor when you are finished.

Career Planning Assignment

For this assignment, you are to consider your long-term career plan by creating and expanding upon your network within your career field. Address any current events in your field for which you may be able to anticipate and plan. Once those things have been done, please write a list of the career goals you hope to accomplish within the next year (short-term) and within the next 2-5 years (long-term).

Also examine where you are in relation to your career goals and write about your plan to achieve the skills and knowledge you need but do not presently have.

Word process your assignment and email it to your professor when you are finished.

Keyboarding Assignment

Caution: this assignment is an "oldie, but a goodie". Many of you will look at this assignment, and think that it is not worth your time. I disagree. Sure, some of you will be going into internships/jobs that do not require the use of a keyboard, whereas some of you will. This assignment is for those of you who will. However, I suggest that you do this assignment even if you are not going into an office-type environment. At the very least, you'll learn a little bit more about yourself.

There are many different skills that are commonly found in workers throughout a variety of businesses. Typing, or keyboarding, is probably the biggest skill that is necessary in a variety of positions at office jobs within those businesses. If the internship/job duties require you to use the computer, interviewers will ask: "how fast you can type or what your typing speed is"? Normally, most of us probably do not know the answer to this question, unless we have timed ourselves, or have taken a keyboarding course and were timed by our instructors.

Luckily, we can turn to the Internet to help us find out how fast we keyboard/type. There are many different online companies that will test your typing speed and ability for free. Two online companies that allow you to test your typing speed for free are: www.typingtest.com and www.abouttyping.com.

You can go to the sites mentioned above, or you can search for one on your own. Either way, keep in mind that these companies are in business to teach you how to type, so they will want to charge you a fee in order for you to use their services. However, they do allow you to take a typing test for free.

For this assignment, go to one of the sites mentioned above, or one that you found on your own, and take a typing test. When you are finished, copy and paste your results into a word file and send the file to your professor.

Final Assignment

At the conclusion of your internship you are to submit a final evaluation of your overall internship experience. The final internship paper should include the following:

1. **A general overview of the internship workplace and your place within it**. Name and describe the organization where your internship took place. Describe your duties and responsibilities and the work you performed on your internship. What did you do every day? Who were some of the other people you met on the internship, and how did you relate to them? What did you learn?

2. **What goals did you have going into your internship?** Did you want to learn a particular skill? Did you want to learn more about the field of work or industry where you performed your internship?

3. **Degree to which your goals were met.** Think about the goals that you set for yourself and discuss how they were or were not met. Describe the reasons why you think that is so. Was it because of the setting, the internship supervisor, the other workers, the nature of the work, the industry, etc.?

4. **Overall internship evaluation.** What did you think of the entire internship experience? Do you feel you have grown professionally? Why or why not? Was it a valuable experience? (Keep in mind that some negative experience can be valuable as well) What did you did you learn about the industry in which you interned? Is this a field where you can see yourself developing a career?

5. **Opinions.** What did you like most about your internship? What did you like least? What should have been included? Excluded? Was there anything you learned in the course that helped you prepare you for anything on your internship? What changes, if any, would you make to the internship course? How valuable were the classroom assignments in preparing and helping you in securing and performance of the internship?

Also remember to have your internship supervisor fill out the Intern Rating Sheet in the back of the workbook.

Please note that this report is due at the final class meeting. Any papers handed in late, or at the final exam, will result in a lower grade!

Internship Proposal Form

For students who must obtain their own internship

This document is intended as a formal agreement among _____ (Intern), _____ (Faculty Supervisor), and _____ (Site Supervisor), concerning a 3-credit internship to be performed during the _____ semester of 20____ at _____ (Name of the Organization).

The objective of the internship is to supplement the intern's general theoretical knowledge of _____ (subject area) that has been gained through academic course work with a practical work experience. The internship objective will be achieved by the intern's performing the following specific duties:

4) _____
_____

5) _____
_____

6) _____
_____

(You may use the back of this form if necessary)

The internship will begin on _____ and conclude on _____. The intern will work for a total of ____ hours. The intern will maintain a daily journal documenting the duties performed. Upon completion of the internship, the intern will submit a paper summarizing his or her activities according to the course requirements.

The site supervisor will directly or indirectly supervise the internship activities, and evaluate the intern's performance using the Intern Evaluation Form provided.

The grade for the internship will be assigned by the faculty supervisor and will be based upon the following components and weights as specified by the supervising faculty member.

5) Classroom/Online Course Component   ____%
6) Site supervisor evaluation   ____%
7) Exams   ____%
8) Other:_____   ____%

_____   _____   _____
(Faculty Supervisor Signature)   (Date)   (Print Site Supervisor Name)

_____   _____   _____
(Intern signature)   (Date)   (Site Supervisor signature)   (Date)

Internship Pledge

I, _____ (Print your name) understand that the internship professor is to place me, or for me to place myself, in a working environment in an industry that matches my academic training. What I get out of the internship is up to me.

I understand that the internship is a bridge between school and the world of work. We learn from the experience, and not all experiences are perfect and wonderful.

I understand that my internship supervisor will expect me to behave like an educated, young adult. His/her evaluation will largely determine my grade. If I have a problem speaking, writing, or with simple math, then this will impact in the type of work that I am assigned to do.

I understand that I am to keep my word.

> I must spend at least 100 hours in the field. (In some cases more)
> I must be on time.
> I must dress properly.
> I must ask questions when unsure.
> I must call if I am unable to go to my internship.

I understand that if I do not keep my word, I will be wasting my time and not complete the course requirements.

I understand that all internships are not created equally and some of the work might be mundane at times.

I understand that an intern is not the President of the company but a newcomer to the organization.

I understand that I must be pro-active and politely speak up for more learning opportunities.

I understand that I may have to keep a journal of my experiences during the internship.

I understand that if I have any problems, at any time, and cannot speak with my internship supervisor, I will call, or meet with, my professor for advice immediately.

I understand that I must be flexible and work hard.

I understand that although completing my hours may be a burden, I am responsible for completing them, no later than the last day to file a grade change form for an INC which usually occurs in the middle of the semester following my internship class.

I understand that my professor may be using his/her personal contacts to place me at an internship, and everything I do is a reflection of my professor, my school and myself. Ruining an internship contact will result in an automatic failure in the course.

Signature:_____
Your signature indicates that you understand and agree to all of the above.

Student Internship Information Form

Name: _____

Email address: _____

Semester and Year: _____

Cell/Telephone Number: _____

What Borough do you live in? _____
Do you own a car? _____

Are you already working? Yes   No   If so, where? _____
Do you intend on doing your internship this semester? Yes   No
If not, then when do you intend on doing your internship?_____

List the top three industries you would like to work in: (For example, hotels, marketing, etc.)

    1. _____
    2. _____
    3. _____

List at least two academic courses you have taken that correspond to the industries you would like to intern in. (For example: Front Office Operations, Principles of Marketing)

    1. _____
    2. _____

List the skills that you possess which will enable you to be successful in your internship:

_____
_____
_____
_____

Please describe yourself and your career goals? List any information you would like your internship supervisor to know about you.

_____
_____
_____
_____
_____

For School use only:
Placement (Organization): _____
Internship supervisor: _____
Phone number: _____

Internship Log

Name of Intern (Student): _____

Organization/Internship location: _____

Date	Day of the Week	Number of Hours	Duties Performed

_____   _____

Signature of Internship Supervisor   Date

Internship Evaluation Form

To Internship Supervisors:

Thank you for allowing our student to be an intern at your organization. As part of his/her grade, we ask that you fill out the following evaluation forms. The first form is a rating sheet wherein we ask that you rate the student-intern's performance on a variety of different criteria. The performance evaluation criteria for the rating sheet is as follows:

- Excellent: Exceptional performance in fulfilling the requirements
- Good: More than frequently meets and exceeds the minimum requirements
- Average: Regularly meets and occasionally exceeds the minimum requirements
- Poor: Very rarely met the minimum requirements, lack of interest
- Failure: Failed to meet the minimum requirements
- Not Applicable: the internship did not require the student-intern to perform any duties that correspond to the specified criteria

In addition to the rating sheet, we ask for a short written narrative evaluating the student-intern's performance. Your observations in regard to the following would be most appreciated:

1. The student-intern's strong points
2. The student-intern's weak points
3. Your opinion of the student-intern's potential in his/her chosen career field

Finally, we ask that you send the forms back, in a timely manner, to the student-intern's professor via regular mail, or you may place the evaluation forms in a sealed envelope and give to the student to return to us.

Once again, thank you for your commitment in contributing to the professional advancement of our students. We truly appreciate all of the time you have invested in our students and our program.

Intern Rating Sheet

Name of Intern (Student): _____

Company/Organization: _____

Semester and Year: _____

Professor: _____

Internship Supervisor: Please use the chart below in evaluating this student's field experience in your organization. Place an X or checkmark in the box that best represents the student's performance in the stated criteria. Thank you.

Criteria	Excellent	Good	Average	Poor	Failure	Not applicable
Productivity: use of time & facilities, volume of work, planning and follow through.						
Quality of work and leadership: Organization, thoroughness, planning						
Relationship with clientele: respect, insight, effectiveness, courtesy						
Communications: ability to communicate effectively with clientele & other staff members, ability to secure acceptance of ideas, consideration of other viewpoints						
Writing ability: degree of skill to express thought on paper, report projects						
Responsibility: ability to meet schedules, follow though, attention to instructions						
Independent functioning: ability to perform without constant supervision & to function constructively on own initiative						
Attendance and Punctuality: regularity of attendance, promptness in reporting absence/lateness						
Attitude toward learning: interest in learning opportunities, desires to learn about various functions and operations of the company						
Judgment: possesses common sense, evaluates problems before making decisions, is logical, practical and tactful						
Application skills: possesses and applies skills commensurate with academic status						

_____   _____   _____   _____

Name of Rater   Date   Signature of Rater   Date